FLOOD PATTERNS

FLOOD PATTERNS

Poems by

Jessica Gigot

Antrim House

Simsbury, Connecticut

Library of Congress Control Number: 2015903359

ISBN: 978-1-936482-84-9

First Edition, 2015

Printed & bound by United Graphics, LLC

Book design by Rennie McQuilkin

Front cover oil painting (detail from "Estuary Farm")
by Kris Ekstrand Molesworth
www.krisekstrand.com

Author photograph by Dean Luce

Antrim House
860.217.0023
AntrimHouse@comcast.net
www.AntrimHouseBooks.com
21 Goodrich Road, Simsbury, CT 06070

for my mother and grandmother

ACKNOWLEDGMENTS

Grateful acknowledgment to the editors of the following publications in which certain poems in this volume first appeared, some in earlier versions:

Floating Bridge Press Review, Pontoons Sections, numbers 5 & 6: "Owl Speak," "Garden Doctrine: Peony & Rose"

Poetry Northwest (v. 9, # 2): "Funeral Dress," "Saint Kateri"

In addition, I wish to thank my previous poetry mentors (Karen Holmberg, Jeanine Hathaway, and Jeanne Murray Walker), as well as my poetry cohort. I am also grateful to the Helen R. Whiteley Center for my 2014 residency.

TABLE OF CONTENTS

Epigraph / ix

I. TERRITORY

II. KINDRED

III. WHAT IS FOUND

IV. WHAT IS LEARNED

They know what has happened to them in past floods and are more fearful of what could happen to them in a really large flood at present, or sometime in the near future.

Report on Skagit River Flood Control Hearing, 1961

FLOOD PATTERNS

I. TERRITORY

Territory

: a field of inquiry
: an area often including a nesting or denning
site and a variable foraging range that is occupied
by an animal or group of animals

When Grandmother visited
From her familiar cul-de-sac
She looked at me and said
"This is your *territory*."

I place root remains and sheep hides
In piles of decay, a wild alchemy
Of epochs that transforms fodder
Into sweet silt under foot.

My work now is not just to love it
And all its verdant greening,
But to stay knee-deep in muck,
Always looking up.

Owl Speak

She hoots, "I'm awake, are you?"
Words in between rhythms.
Owl is a guide for how to watch
Hollow as an old snag standing amongst
Vine maple limbs. Listen, like the vole clan
Quivering under remnants of exposed nest
Turned by ploughed clods of farmland.

Your story is here, in the barley
And the salty drift of morning.
And here is all we know.

Flood Patterns

Skagit Delta

Nobody wants to lose land.
God plays with the light until
The sky becomes empty and dark.
A storm trembles in the mountain
Echoing thunder.

This river can run high
As glaciers thread down to thick streams.
When the land was half-marsh, the fields
Knew only flood.

Our truths are ready to spill over the rim
Every time the river rises again.

Recession Limb

The water pulls back slowly, leaving
Cemented soil and reeds scattered.
No one can remember the last time
This place flooded. We are counting
Our blessings like ravens.
Whether it is a truce or a dare
That finger wants to come closer
Each time we sandbag it away.

Samish River Dike

To be rooted is perhaps the most needed and
least recognized need of the human soul.

– Simone Weil

Crafted by the Dutch settlers
In a massive movement of earth,
This floodplain was molded like porcelain.

As I walk along the dike, I wonder
Who made the first imprint on this loam?

In the reeds there is a gentle murmur
But no voice.
In the hush there is a gentle prayer
But no answer.

In the deep clay along the bank,
Only a cast of my perishable stance.

Ditch

This is man-made land.
Soil scoured to escape
A brackish past. These veins
Save us while they sell every
Story to the sea. We forget
Our fear of flooding sometimes.
We forget there was ever fear
At all.

Tide Gates

Opening, closing, regulating seawater.
These rivers are not home to everyone.
They only let in what they know.
Saltwater intrusion is death
To the Jack-Be-Littles
But fresh life to migrating spawn.
If doors could be windows
I would see the how of its mixing.
Grievances spawn gossip
While fisherman and farmers
Hold claim to the mystery of current.

Blight, Rot

The tuber is safe underground,
Nested, seed-like, almost sprouted
Unless decorated zoospores enter lenticels,
Letting white downy strands melt the fields.

The same goes for the tender drupe.
Oopspores awaken and permeate the crown,
Streaks extend to the tip of the cane, fading any
Hope for blossom and the sweet rewards of summer.

And that is why the farmers pray, he says,
Anointing the crops with their spray.

Counting Salmon

May 5, 2014

"I don't believe in magic. I believe in the sun and the stars,
the water, the tides, the floods, the owls, the hawks flying,
the river running, the wind talking. They're measurements."

– Billy Frank, Jr.

Decades have gone by fighting.
Birth rite, treaty rights, half
Of the allowable harvest.

Chinook swim in long, unfathomable ellipses.
The beauty of their travels cannot be measured.

While I sit and watch this river
By my house, I lose track of data,
And experimental design.

I remember that the salmon only know the smell
Of the memory banks that beckon them home.

Daffodil Truck

Bundled in crates, stacked ten high
By five wide. joyful yellow heads
Bobble and nod. In April, flowers
Are picked fast for Easter bouquets,
Cross-greening ceremonies.
As I follow down the main road
The truck dithers across uneven
Back roads. Picker's rubber hands
Fasten to wooden side grates
For safety or for prayer.
Loose stems pour out like water.
The day is far from over.

Louisa Ann Conner

Your husband bought you a millinery shop,
Hats and such. You did what you could
To prosper. Now this channel town seals your name,
First non-native lady set here by fate.

I drive by your namesake church, white as cream,
Pointed above the town's natural ridgeline.
You once paddled through rivers and slough
To raise money for this church.

The reservation that lies between here and the sea
Seems worlds away from the stained glass view.
Sometimes, Louisa, I try to remember
What this valley was like before I landed
And decided it was home.

II. KINDRED

Rock Tumbler

My mother likes to polish rocks.
I can hear them clink together
Releasing rhythm and rage
From their time at sea.
I am napping on the couch
As she wanders outside
For a smoke. In the garden
She inspects her peonies and mole
Traps like a dutiful field marshal.
When I wake, she is upstairs
Putting away glasses, balancing
Her checkbook. She never thought
She would be alone at this age.
Then again, neither did I.
We sit and drink wine together
Play hand after hand of double solitaire
Watching the rough agates of daylight
Soften into dark.

Motherhood

When the lilacs come back
I remember that I was born,
That there was a robin's nest
Outside my mother's bedroom window
As she waited to count my toes.
Now her hands rest on her stomach
Tangled in contemplation
As if I am still in there.
Her fingers are woven together
Like a fisherman's net as she tries
One more time, to offer advice.

Recovery Room

I am camped on the pullout couch in the den
waiting for Grandma to wake. These mornings
are precious like Auntie Mar's turquoise.
Grandma grabs her favorite mug and crosswords.
I slip into the kitchen to sit beside her. I am
ten not thirty. Her wool cap covers her last
feathers of hair. The coffee percolates like a slow
heartbeat. Under the genesis of sun and cardinals
we share this solace. One morning, our respite,
before the next nurse arrives.

Learning Harmony

Fields crusted with snow, sagebrush stillness
Fills the Oregon high desert 's short days.

No more Christmas carols, just the old tunes.
My aunt plays the chords, I find my note

And sing a third above, tenor harmony:
No more sweet caress hello emptiness.

I remember the red of Grandma's sumac and cardinal
Blazing against the afterglow of Wisconsin snowfall.

She would pat the dishes dry, listen from above the sink.

The tea leaves settle in the pot
And we start over from the beginning,

Finding that tender space between our voices
That binds them and reminds us of her:

One deep raven call, echoing gracefully
Between pine and tamarack.

The Carbon Cycle

On this planet, there is a sink
Of carbon that is untraceable –
Two billion tons gone missing.
By science, the models do not
Match up. A mysterious inhale with no
Exhale. A furtive lung filling underground.

She was found dead at the edge of campus.
I didn't have room to cry under the fear
That I could be her someday.

Some cultures believe that breathing
Together is sacred. Trees fall and we feel pressure
In some deep vacuole, intentional cellular
Respiration, a ceremony of shared air.

I am imagining her on all fours,
Taking small gasps of oxygen
In between the poison she ingested.
The detritus she studied, a life's work,
Remained just an empty gasp after all.
When we succeed we are never close enough.

Saint Kateri

Uprooted from her mother earth,
Transplant to pagan soil,
Marred face could not hide her mirth,
As nimble hands did toil.

– Marlene McCauley

Her third miracle was in Ferndale.
They placed pieces of her fractured bone
Over the young boy's skin-shredded body.
The luster of bacteria, furiously multiplying,
Froze in the kind darkness.

Now she stands in metal
Welcoming artists and cowboys
To the Cathedral of St. Francis,
Boots worn high to reflect
Late afternoon desert light.

We will remember to
Remember her, a fair flower,
Before the bleeding and pain.
Her face one pure spark
Falling back to the earth.

III. WHAT IS FOUND

Birth of a Naturalist

She watched and she listened as each cardinal
And finch visited the feeder, suet swinging
For pileated woodpeckers,
Crumbs scattered for wild turkey.
Her gentle brush would dip between
Pigment and water before deciding on lines.
Even the possum placed his tender
Pink pads on the porch glass
To beg for her last strokes of attention.

Pretending To Be St. Francis

The sheep greet me at the fence
As I carry grain from the shed
To the wooden feeder.
I am groggy and waking up slowly.
I feel them sensing me out
Of their black dash eyes –
A bleat, and then a nudge
Behind my knee.
I strew barley and oats,
Jam the racks with hay squares.
They chomp and swallow
Many loud *thankyous*.
Sometimes I feel their gratitude
Sometimes I just see breath.

Feeding Eagles

Three, four, seven
Sit rigid on the fir.
Bald-capped adult,
Speckled juvenile.
A golden swoops
By on the breeze.

There is a ritual of leaving
Fish and oyster remnants out at five.

I scour the horizon
With my camera, looking
For the best shot of talons.
Wild can still be scintillating
And wild, even when
The food is free.

Hummingbird

I am still searching for a nest
Tight as a silver dollar, woven
Shallow atop branches. I never knew
Eggs could be so small. But
I am not afraid for you, new mother.
I know your cache is safe. How
Can such delicate beauty ever
Be touched or tarnished? How can
It ever be found?

Garden Doctrine:
Peony & Rose

Sarah Bernhardt comes
By surprise each year.
Tight fitting, light hue
With a multitude of petals.
They scatter, or stick to
The head of Buddha
In what feels like
A single moment
Before they are gone.

Heirloom, nameless rose
Unfurls in stages from
Green bud to open story.
And once she starts talking
You can hear her royal chime,
Smell her scent for centuries.
One by one her red pieties
Float by Saint Francis as he
Prays for renewal.

When Plants Talk

They are not whimpering, but bowing
To wind. Open stomata, silent voices
That chant in leaf rustle, roar in blossom
And stop you in your tracks.
Steadfast as balsam root
Under sage brush, pioneering
As blood root under shagbark hickory,
They take notice all the time, point directions
With each emerging petiole and leaflet.
It is the listening that is the hard part
And faith enough to heed.

Harvesting Nettles on Good Friday

Hunched under the willow
I rest between gloved bunches.
Their burn caught my arm on fire
So I pause for cool winds.
These plants come back every year
In the same patch by the gate.
I admire their alternating leaves
Like a verdant cross. At home,
I boil off the innocent spikes
Until there is only true skin.
The burden is not the harvest,
But waiting for this medicine
To strain and cool
And heal.

Amelanchier

Your fruit was the first sustenance
To pioneers so they called you serviceberry.
The Cree call you *Misaaskwatoomina,*
Berries that become pemmican cakes
Cut with fat and meat.
Saskatoon is the name they farm
Now in Alberta, but you are still
Juneberry back East – the namesake month
When your blues come on in splendor,
A homely shrub, haloed in tart taste.
If only I could remember
To look beneath the trees,
I would see you always offering.

Erna's Notes on Gooseberry

Eat the berries fresh, but never store them.
Boil the roots and drink the infusion for
*   sore throat.*

The plants and their uses are often forgotten
Except in her middens of notes.

When we forget to see their pink
Blossoms and red fruit, we forget
To see ourselves.

IV. WHAT IS LEARNED

Falling Farm

for Georgie

As the last leaves gather
Around the base of the chestnut
Geese return to the westward field.
They coolly comb the vacant rows
Once corn, now stubble.
Snow spans its wings across the hills
Like angels; the glossy glow of dawn
Shines prophetic on leaf and hoof.
Donkey, sheep, gentle herb
Stand against the frigid dark –
It's doggedness that does it
And faith in the next spring.
Let our bevy glide into winter
With no wisps of despair.
Let us celebrate every solemn
Slap of rime and remember –
A fire breathes beneath the cold.

Her Quiet Bounty

Beside the warped pavement
Muddied in tire print mesh,
A blue heron arrows its beak
Into the algae and brown.

Tined snow lines break
From the feathered fog.
Underneath, white swans
Bathe in field sea reflections
Of distant peaks.

Bare canes rainbow over stillness
Awaiting the subtle pulse of blossom,
While chickweed swathes the
Broken mounds of tender loam.

Soon the lookers will come in droves
Seeking the valley's berries and bulbs,
Making her blush summer praises.
But before these days begin to swell
While the quiet bounty lurks,
I am beholden to the depths
Of her winter.

Winter Squash

I roast acorn squash in the oven
For days. The steam comes up
Through the burners,
The flesh falls back in silence.
I've waited all winter for this fiery
February night. Despite your tender
Green back and steep gullies
You are magnificently dense.
A hidden boon from last fall
That is ready to give
And tastes like gold.

Lessons from Borsht

Washing fresh beets
From the farm, quartering them
While the juices stain wood
And finger prints.
Mauve, plunged
Into boiling water.
I wait for the familiar grouse
Of truck and gravel.
I move the barbicans of
Old crosswords.
Place bowls and candles
As offerings
To an imperfect god.

I can wait.
I always wait.

Red steam swells
Over dish stacks, to blender.
I look at the green fields,
The light across a place
I want to be forever.
I am startled by the door.
The loosening lid

Hurls pieces of my heart
Across walls, floors,
Thighs and neck.
My hands dripping beet,
Yours soiled in regret.

Wash your hands, if you can.
Dinner will be late
And I am not hungry anymore.

The Art of Stirring Risotto

I was 32 when I started cooking, up until
then I just ate.   – Julia Child

I put the fork close to my mouth,
Sniff the steam for spice,
Breathe away the threat of burn.

Dishes like this take
Time and endurance.
We steal the frail anthers
Of saffron at sunrise with tweezers,
Smuggle chanterelles in darkness
Down switchbacks.

Life for the epicure
Is everything, including
The long, hungry wait.

Hunting and Gathering

He is learning to fish
On the Samish, with the old timers
And the girl from the goat dairy.

He has not caught one yet,
But the hurt of wanting
Stays him on the bank
Until the last lure
Eddies or the
Pink sky folds into purple.

I am home, canning
Peaches and watching
That same horizon,
Now the color of
This fruit flesh.
A trade from
The farmer's market
When no one sold out.

I'll start dinner
When he comes back. Or
Maybe we will just
Go to the bar
For some red cabbage
And steak.

I can do the apples
Later, and maybe
Just freeze the sauce.

He returns. An empty bucket.
I set the tongs
On the cutting board,
Grab the keys
And go. For now,
While we still can afford it.

Laboratory, Radio

I count nematodes
Under the tiny slide squares.
Each square represents
The total, times a hundred.
I took them from the soil,
From their lives under roots.

A visiting scientist
In a laboratory where
The radio stays on,
I hear Oregon
(One, two, three)
Public Broadcasting's
(Four, five, six)
Special feature
sex trafficking.

Click, click, click –
I try to hide in the eyepiece.
Now we talk with a
Former prostitute that was
Sold by her mother.
Thirteen,
Thirteen,
Thirteen.

False Start

Eliot said April is the cruelest month.
Fresh buds fall limp under a sneak freeze,
cower under emboldened hail.

Millay says April comes like an idiot
Babbling and strewing flowers.
I am hit upside the head with first
Petals, then a yellow lingering infection
That seeps from my throat like tree sap.

I am ripe for spring, but unable to blossom
Or shed my flannel cocoon.
I coddle a warm mug and wait –
Remembering that April is April every time.

Indian Plum

Your first green leaves
Want the warmth of spring.
I remember seeing you
On those bitter morning walks
Outside my cabin, when I lived alone
With one strong, grey cat.
I was waiting all winter for your
White blossoms, spring signals
To ease my cold heart sting.
Even though I moved out of the woods
I still need a taste of solitude,
I still need your tenderness.

Stalking the Poet Laureate on Retreat

A river otter staggers between our cabins
Gentle brown and willowy, headed straight
For the ease of saltwater. It doesn't see me,
But instead spirits along a habitual path.

In her cabin window the poet is still, staring
Beyond the island's cerulean edge. I huff
At my white, glaring screen and cold tea.

I envy these solitary creatures –
Both doing what they do
Each day without doubt.

Altitude Alignment

My plane rises from the cloud layer,
Greeting the mountain in her grandeur
Crowned in morning light,
Boasting a new stole of snow.
I watch a subtle arc of umber
Spread across the moon.
I, the only witness
As eclipse and majesty meet
At eye level.

Making Ceremony by the Sea

Atlantic

A fan of light straddles
Open water and rocky slopes.
A marriage of a Mexican
And a Greek on a
Moss covered island.
She is married by
Her brother who announces
"You may now kiss my sister."
We chant sea air vows
Into September's elusive swales
And clink to a blue moon toast.

Pacific

Sitting on hay bales
We look out at the Sound,
The Olympics and
Exsiccated pasture.
A Haida button blanket
Is draped over cedar logs
Laid between a vibraphone

And a stone-rimmed fire pit.
His wife, an old student
And a men's club friend
Speak their respects
Before we all stand
To send his bear spirit
Beyond a new moon sunset.

Funeral Dress

The first time I wore this dress, I was singing
At a funeral. Now I am waiting for a table.
This town has a namesake mountain saloon,
A hardware store and one fancy bistro.
We eat roasted tomatoes, share poached pears,
I nibble on bread, you straighten your tie.
The large plates arrive and distract us
Like the children we haven't had yet.
In the walk back to the car I thought I was grieving
But you grab my hand and I thank you with a kiss.
We are not dead yet, we are just approaching the foothills.

Apology

We all fall down.
We all weep sometimes.
Today we give thanks for orange,
For ice, and then warm hands
Around our waists.

The sky tells pretty truths,
While the solace of twilight
Spreads into my sleeves and collar.

We are all right.
We have felt this pain before.
Trust and more trust,
Rising up from the space
Between field and sunset.

ABOUT THE AUTHOR

Jessica Gigot, Ph.D., M.F.A, is a poet, farmer, teacher and musician. Her small farm in Bow, WA – Harmony Fields – grows herbs, lamb and produce. She offers educational and art workshops through her Art in the Barn series, and has an academic background in horticulture and plant pathology. Jessica has lived in the Skagit Valley for over ten years and is deeply connected to the artistic and agricultural communities that coexist in the region. Her writing has been published in the *Floating Bridge Press Review* and *Poetry Northwest*.

This book is set in Garamond Premier Pro, which had its genesis in 1988 when type-designer Robert Slimbach visited the Plantin-Moretus Museum in Antwerp, Belgium, to study its collection of Claude Garamond's metal punches and typefaces. During the mid-fifteen hundreds, Garamond—a Parisian punch-cutter—produced a refined array of book types that combined an unprecedented degree of balance and elegance, for centuries standing as the pinnacle of beauty and practicality in type-founding. Slimbach has created an entirely new interpretation based on Garamond's designs and on compatible italics cut by Robert Granjon, Garamond's contemporary.

To order additional copies of this book
or other Antrim House titles, contact the publisher at

Antrim House
21 Goodrich Rd., Simsbury, CT 06070
860.217.0023, AntrimHouse@comcast.net
or the house website (www.AntrimHouseBooks.com).

•

On the house website
in addition to information on books
you will find sample poems, upcoming events,
and a "seminar room" featuring supplemental biography,
notes, images, poems, reviews, and
writing suggestions.